Blast Off
to 1st Grade Math

Kindergarten to 1st Grade Transition Math Workbook

GET THE ANSWER KEY

The answer key for this book is available as a free PDF download.

SCAN HERE

Copyright © 2023 EDventure Learning LLC

All rights reserved. This book or any portion thereof may not be reproduced or used in any manner whatsoever without the express written permission of the publisher.

This product is not sponsored or endorsed by the Common Core State Standards Initiative of the National Governors Association Center for Best Practices and the Council of Chief State School Officers.

Printed in the United States of America
ISBN: 978-1-64824-037-9
EDventure Learning LLC
5601 State Route 31 #1296
Clay, NY 13039

www.edventurelearning.com

Email us at hello@edventurelearning.com
Follow us on social media @edventurelearning

This book is part of the **Bridge Builder Learning Series**, designed to help bridge the gap between grade levels. The content in this book is designed to review math from kindergarten and set students up for success in 1st grade.

CONTENTS

Unit 1 Numbers and Counting .... p. 5

Unit 2 Operations .... p. 55

Unit 3 Geometry .... p. 75

Unit 4 Measurement and Data .... p. 95

UNIT 1
5

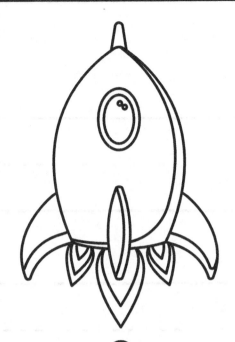

Numbers and Counting

Skill 1 Numbers Up to 10 .... p. 6

Skill 2 Numbers Up to 20 .... p. 16

Skill 3 Numbers Up to 100 .... p. 24

Skill 4 Skip Counting .... p. 38

Skill 5 Place Value .... p. 44

Skill 6 Comparing Numbers .... p. 48

6 — Numbers Up to 10

Trace and write the numbers 1-5.

1 -

2 -

3 -

4 -

5 -

Numbers Up to 10

Trace and write the numbers 6-10.

6

7

8

9

10

8   Numbers Up to 10

Count the bugs. Color in the correct number of boxes.

Numbers Up to 10

9

Count the objects in each group and circle the correct number.

sunglasses (2)	1 **(2)** 3	fish (7) — 5, 6, 8
beach balls (3)	2 3 5	hat (1) — 0, 1, 2
flowers (9)	6 8 9	umbrellas (4) — 4, 5, 6
popsicles (5)	4 5 7	shells (10) — 7, 8, 10

10 — Numbers Up to 10

Count the spots on each ladybug and write the number on the lines.

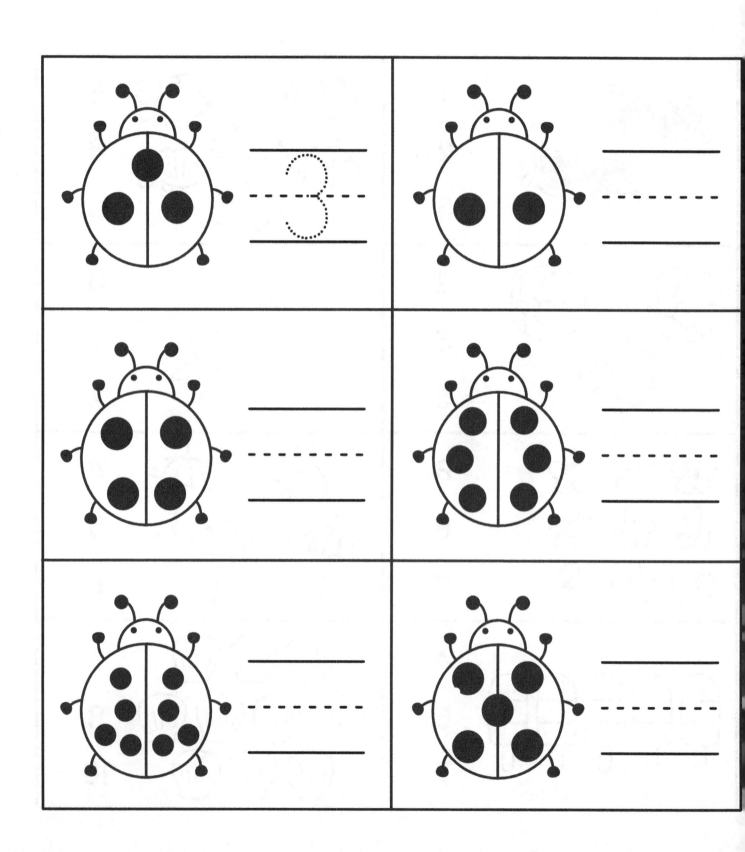

Numbers Up to 10

11

Read the number on each fish and draw that number of bubbles.

12 Numbers Up to 10

Count the shapes. Write the number on the lines.

 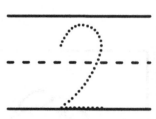

 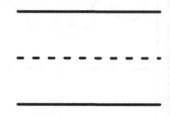

 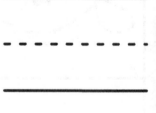

 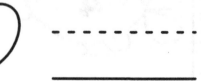

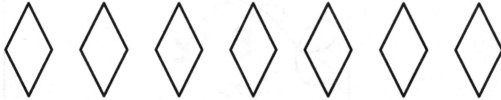 

Numbers Up to 10

Count the shapes. Write the number on the lines.

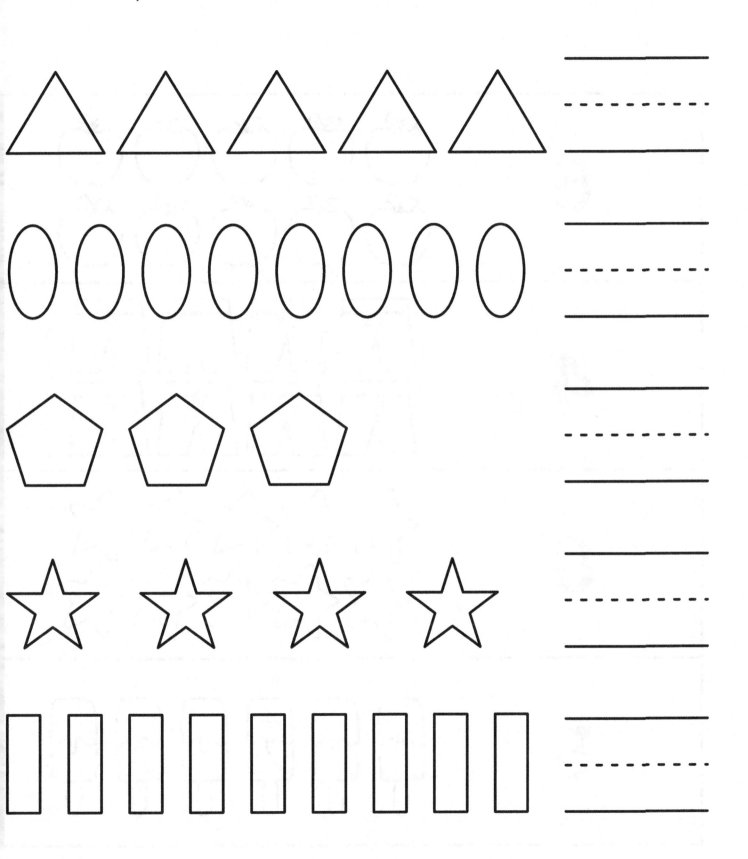

| 14 | **Numbers Up to 10** |

Color the given number of each object.

6	🍎🍎🍎🍎🍎 🍎🍎🍎🍎🍎
4	(8 shorts)
8	(10 stars)
5	(6 popsicles)

Numbers Up to 10

Trace each number and color in that number of spaces in each ten frame.

3

9

7

10

16 — Numbers Up to 20

Trace and write the numbers 11-15.

11 --

12 --

13 --

14 --

15 --

Numbers Up to 20

Trace and write the numbers 16-20.

16 — — — — — — — — — — — — — — —

17 — — — — — — — — — — — — — — —

18 — — — — — — — — — — — — — — —

19 — — — — — — — — — — — — — — —

20 — — — — — — — — — — — — — — —

18   Numbers Up to 20

Count the balls. Color in the correct number of boxes in the ten frames.

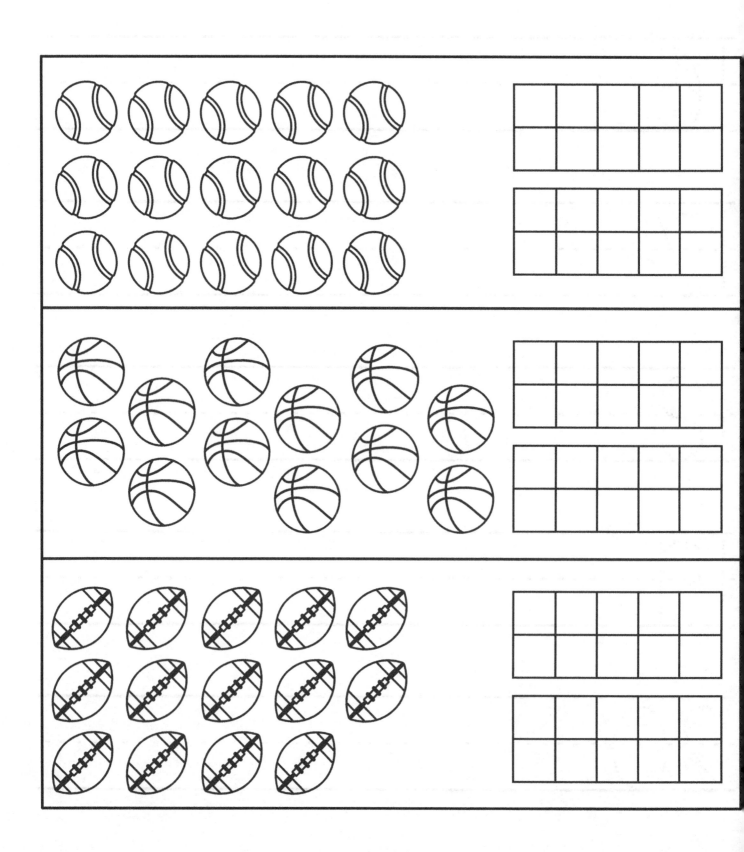

Numbers Up to 20

19

Count the pieces of fruit in each group and circle the correct number.

(apples)	10 **(11)** 12
(apples)	16 18 20
(oranges)	15 17 19
(pears)	13 14 15

20 Numbers Up to 10

Count the shapes. Write the number on the lines.

 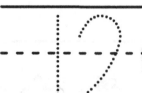

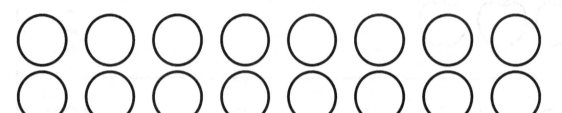

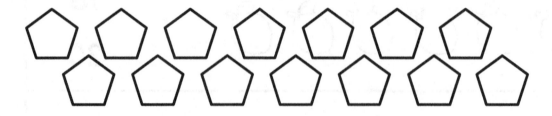

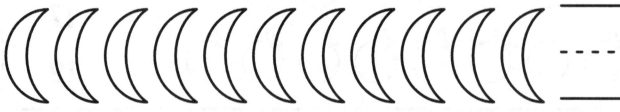

Numbers Up to 10

21

Count the shapes. Write the number on the lines.

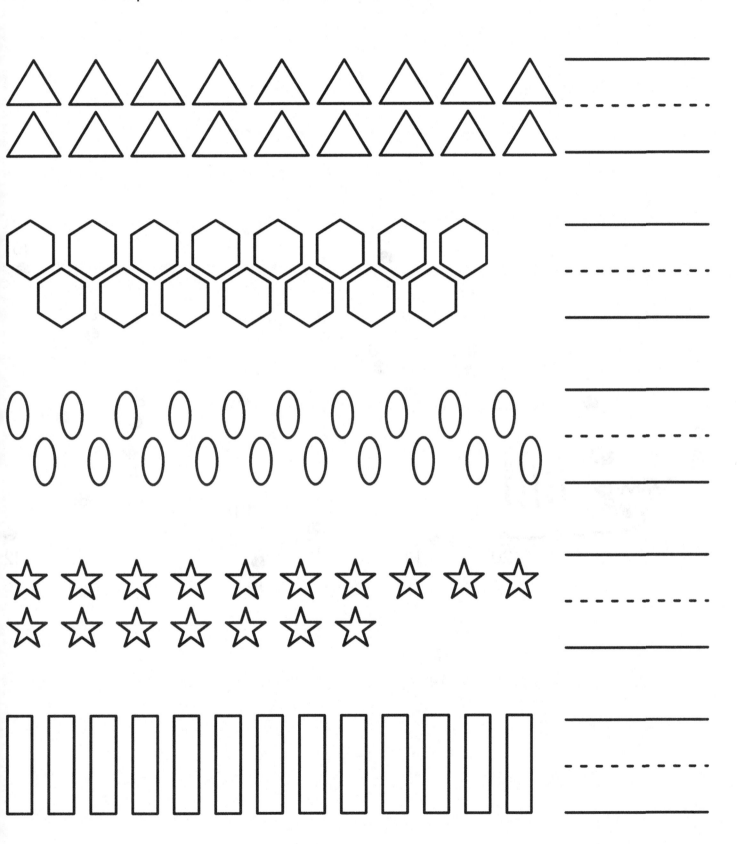

22 | Numbers Up to 20

Connect the dots in order 1-20 to complete the outline. Then color the picture.

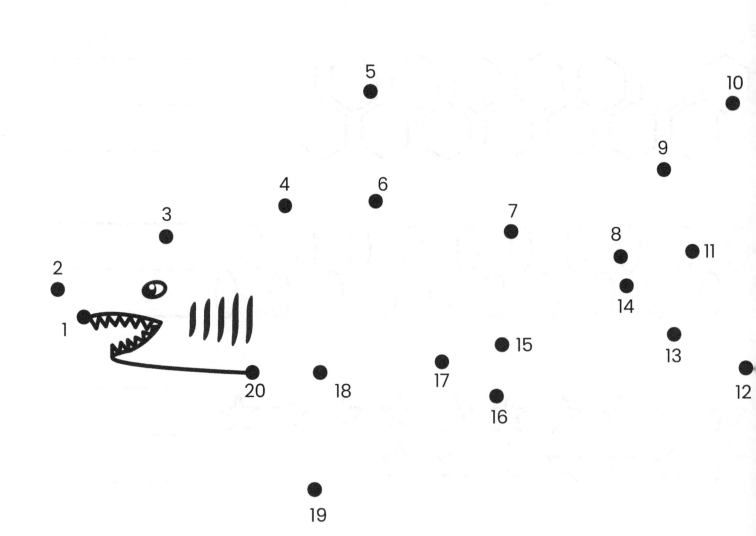

Numbers Up to 20

Count on and fill in the numbers that come next in each series.

Numbers Up to 100

Trace and write the numbers 20-29.

20 21

22 23

24 25

26 27

28 29

Numbers Up to 100

Trace and write the numbers 30-39.

30 .... 31 ....

32 .... 33 ....

34 .... 35 ....

36 .... 37 ....

38 .... 39 ....

26 Numbers Up to 100

Trace and write the numbers 40-49.

40 —————— 41 ——————

42 —————— 43 ——————

44 —————— 45 ——————

46 —————— 47 ——————

48 —————— 49 ——————

Numbers Up to 100

Trace and write the numbers 50-59.

50 ----- 51 -----

52 ----- 53 -----

54 ----- 55 -----

56 ----- 57 -----

58 ----- 59 -----

28   Numbers Up to 100

Trace and write the numbers 60-69.

60 —————————— 61 ——————————

62 —————————— 63 ——————————

64 —————————— 65 ——————————

66 —————————— 67 ——————————

68 —————————— 69 ——————————

Numbers Up to 100

29

Trace and write the numbers 70-79.

70   71

72   73

74   75

76   77

78   79

| 30 | Numbers Up to 100 |

Trace and write the numbers 80-89.

80 ---------- 81 ----------

82 ---------- 83 ----------

84 ---------- 85 ----------

86 ---------- 87 ----------

88 ---------- 89 ----------

Numbers Up to 100

31

Trace and write the numbers 90-100.

90 — — — — 91 — — — —

92 — — — — 93 — — — —

94 — — — — 95 — — — —

96 — — — — 97 — — — —

98 — — — — 99 — — — —

100 — — — — — — — — —

| 32 | | | Numbers Up to 100 | | | | | | |

Fill in the missing numbers from 1 to 100.

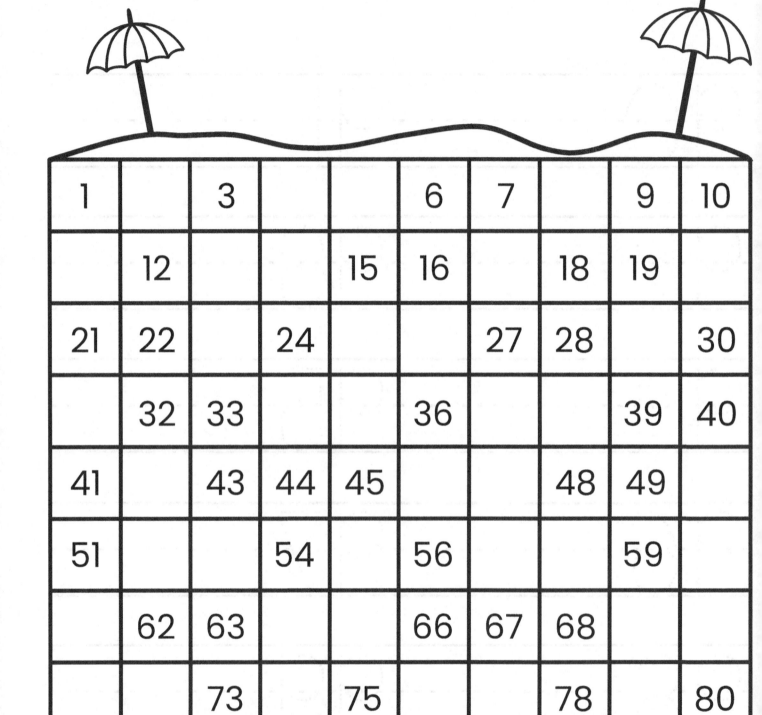

1		3			6	7		9	10
	12			15	16		18	19	
21	22		24			27	28		30
	32	33			36			39	40
41		43	44	45			48	49	
51			54		56			59	
	62	63			66	67	68		
		73		75			78		80
81	82		84			87		89	
		93		95			98		100

Numbers Up to 100

Count on and fill in the numbers that come next in each series.

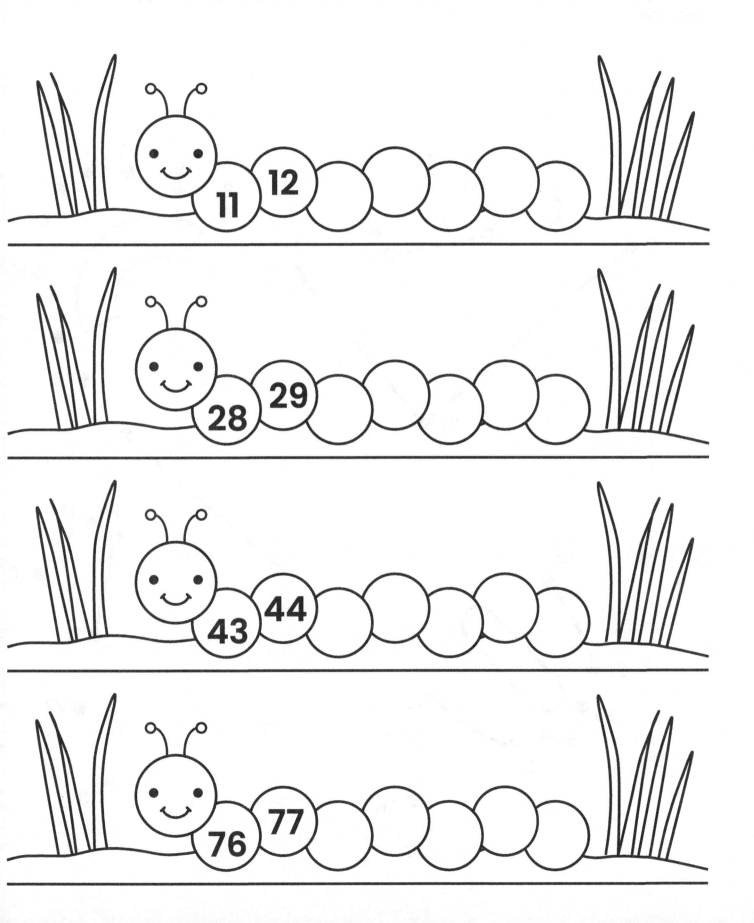

| 34 | Numbers Up to 100 |

Connect the dots in order 1-35 to complete the outline. Then color the picture.

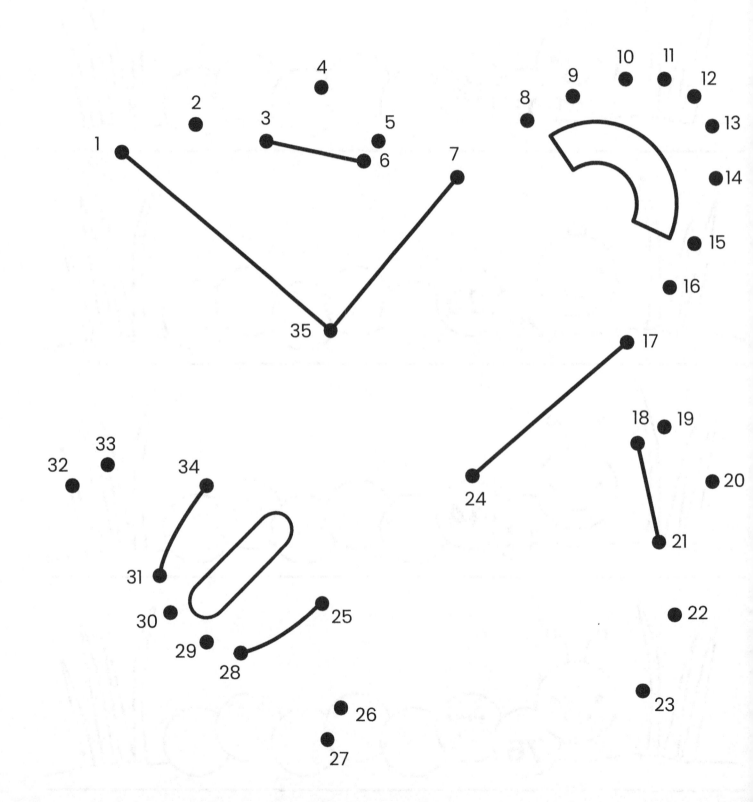

Numbers Up to 100

35

Starting at 1, color the numbers 1-50 in order to make a path out of the maze.

START ↓

	19	4	5	6	7	11	33	47	5
1	2	3	22	31	8	35	28	29	30
8	25	20	11	10	9	13	27	39	31
15	14	13	12	32	4	25	26	18	32
16	29	34	7	22	23	24	46	42	33
17	18	19	20	21	37	10	17	2	34
3	41	38	27	14	45	23	44	40	35
16	24	9	44	43	42	49	38	37	36
50	49	15	45	6	41	40	39	26	21
	48	47	46	36	12	28	43	1	30

↓ **FINISH**

36 Numbers Up to 100

Fill in the missing number on each number line.

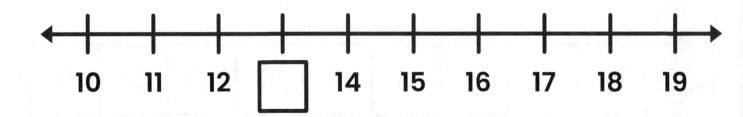

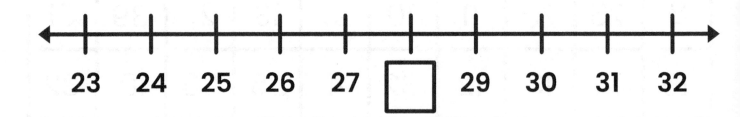

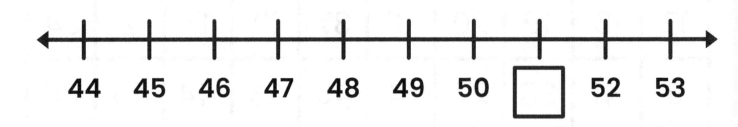

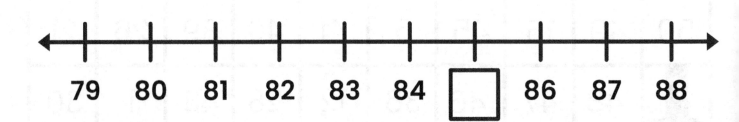

Numbers Up to 100

There are 32 shells inside the bucket and several more outside the bucket. Count forward from 32 to find the total number of shells. Write the answer on the line.

There are 68 pieces of popcorn inside the container and several more outside the container. Count forward from 68 to find the total number of pieces of popcorn. Write the answer on the line.

 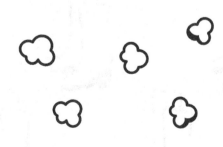

38 Skip Counting

Skip count by twos to find the number of shoes in each group. Write the number on the lines.

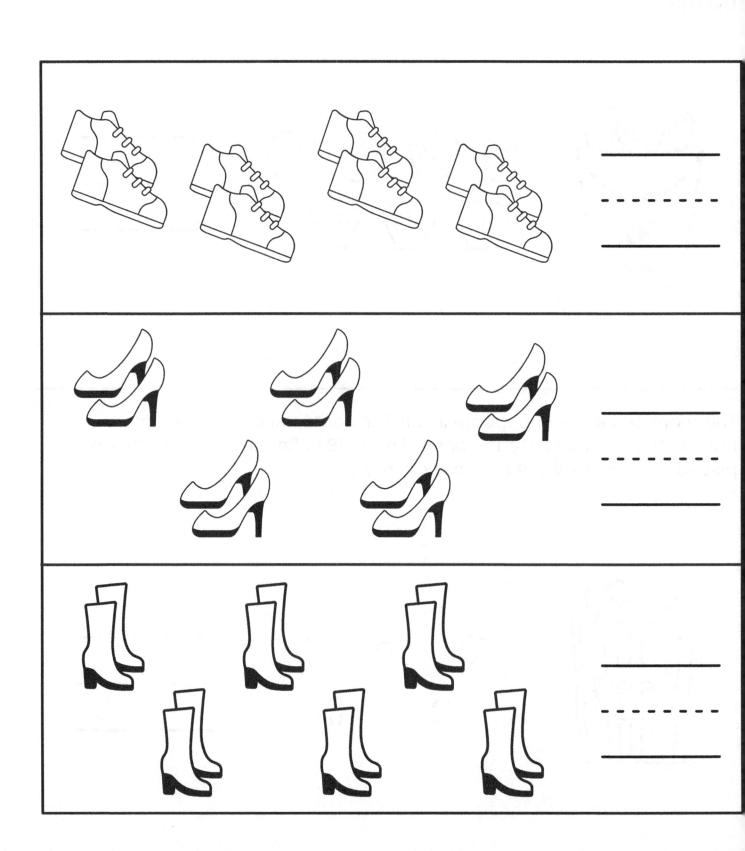

Skip Counting 39

Fill in the missing numbers to count by twos.

Skip Counting

40

Skip count by fives to find the total number of balloons. Write the number on the lines.

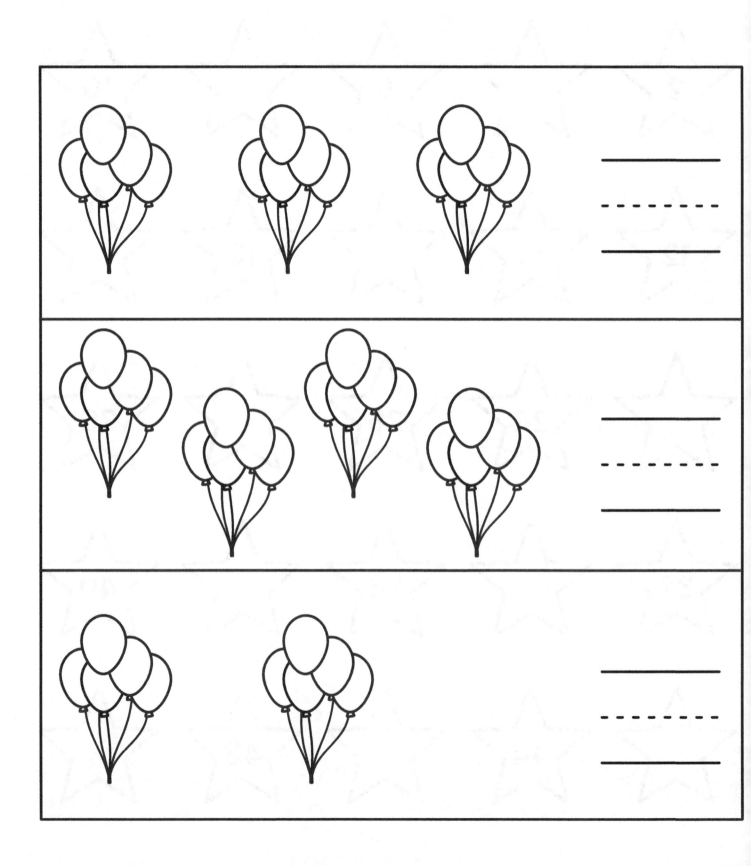

Skip Counting 41

Fill in the missing numbers to count by fives.

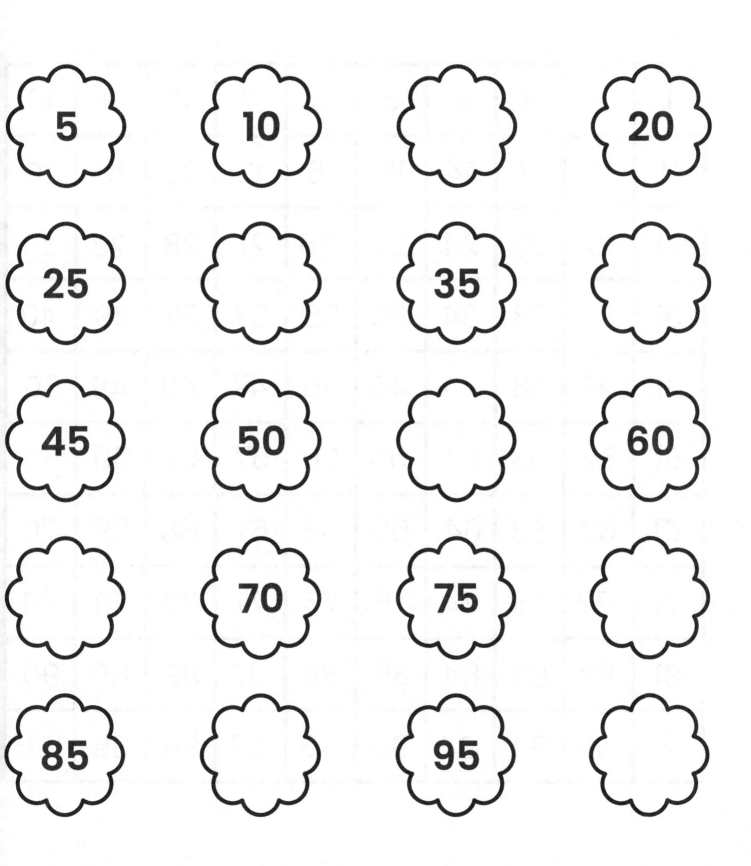

42 Skip Counting

Color the number 10. Count by tens to 100. Color each number as you say it.

1	2	3	4	5	6	7	8	9	10
11	12	13	14	15	16	17	18	19	20
21	22	23	24	25	26	27	28	29	30
31	32	33	34	35	36	37	38	39	40
41	42	43	44	45	46	47	48	49	50
51	52	53	54	55	56	57	58	59	60
61	62	63	64	65	66	67	68	69	70
71	72	73	74	75	76	77	78	79	80
81	82	83	84	85	86	87	88	89	90
91	92	93	94	95	96	97	98	99	100

Skip Counting

43

Write the missing numbers in the empty suns to count by tens.

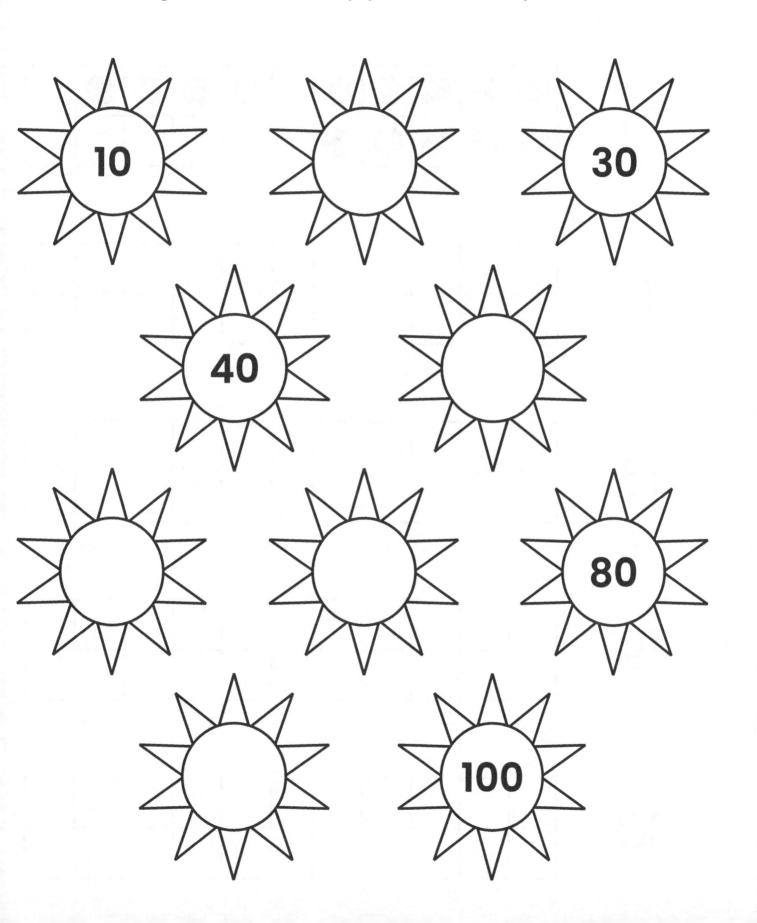

44 Place Value

Draw circles in the ten frames to show each number.

14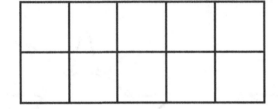

11

16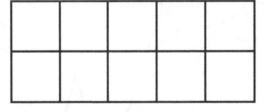

19

13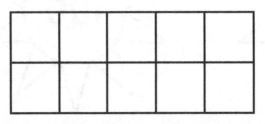

Place Value 45

In each number shown, color the digit in the tens place **BLUE** and the digit in the ones place **GREEN**. Then, color in the number cubes below each digit with the same colors.

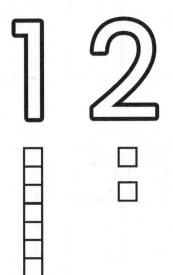
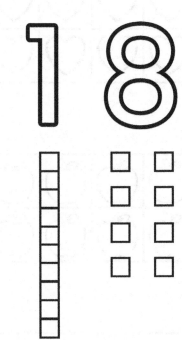
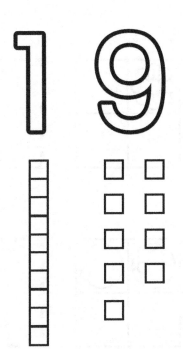
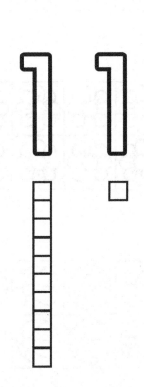

46 Place Value

Find the number of object in each set of ten frames and write it in the box.

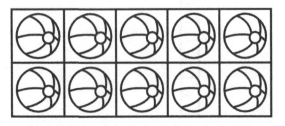 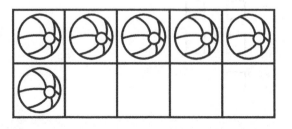

Place Value   47

Use the number of tens and ones to find the total number.

__1__ ten + __3__ ones = __13__

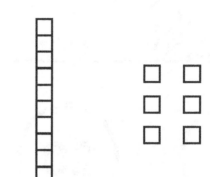

___ ten + ___ ones = ___

___ ten + ___ ones = ___

___ ten + ___ ones = ___

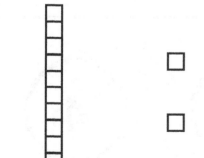

___ ten + ___ ones = ___

___ ten + ___ ones = ___

48 Comparing Numbers

In each pair, color the number that is **GREATER**.

13 20	17 19
11 9	1 3
17 12	5 2
14 18	6 4

Comparing Numbers

49

Draw a line to connect a ball of one type to a ball of the other type. Write the number of each type of ball on the lines. Circle the **LARGER** number.

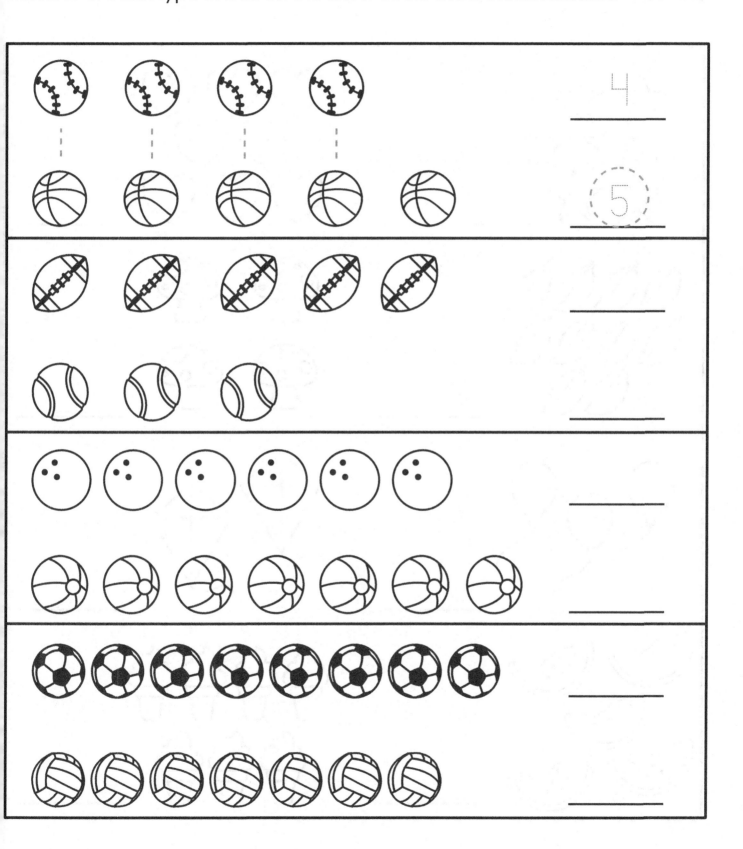

50   Comparing Numbers

Count the objects in each group. Write the number on the line. Circle the **LARGER** number in each pair.

Comparing Numbers   51

In each pair, color the number that is **LESS**.

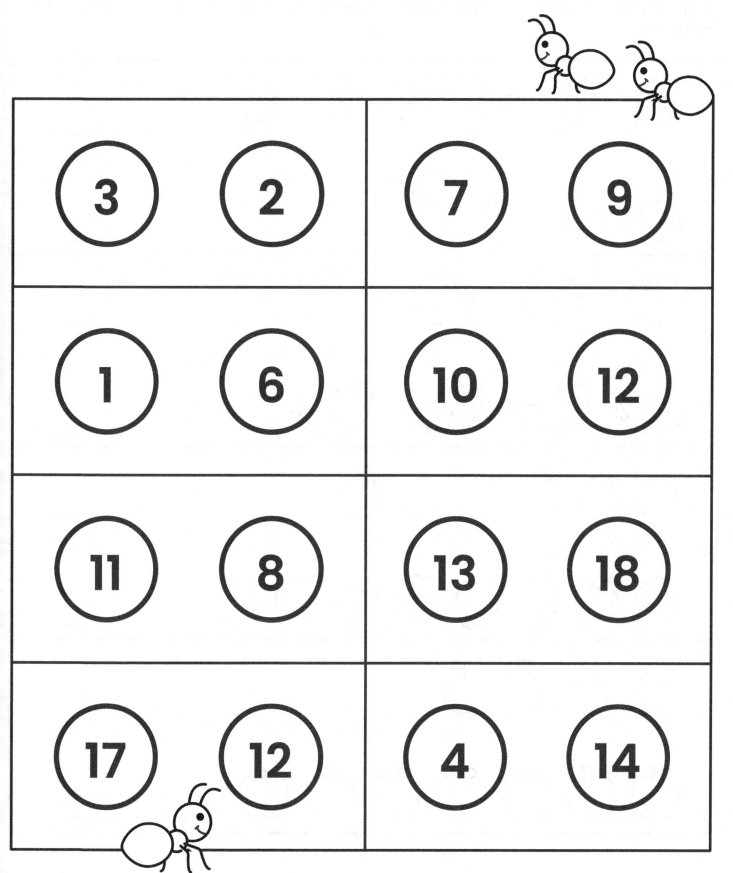

52 Comparing Numbers

Draw a line to connect a piece of one type of food to a piece of the other type. Write the number of each type of food on the lines. Circle the **SMALLER** number.

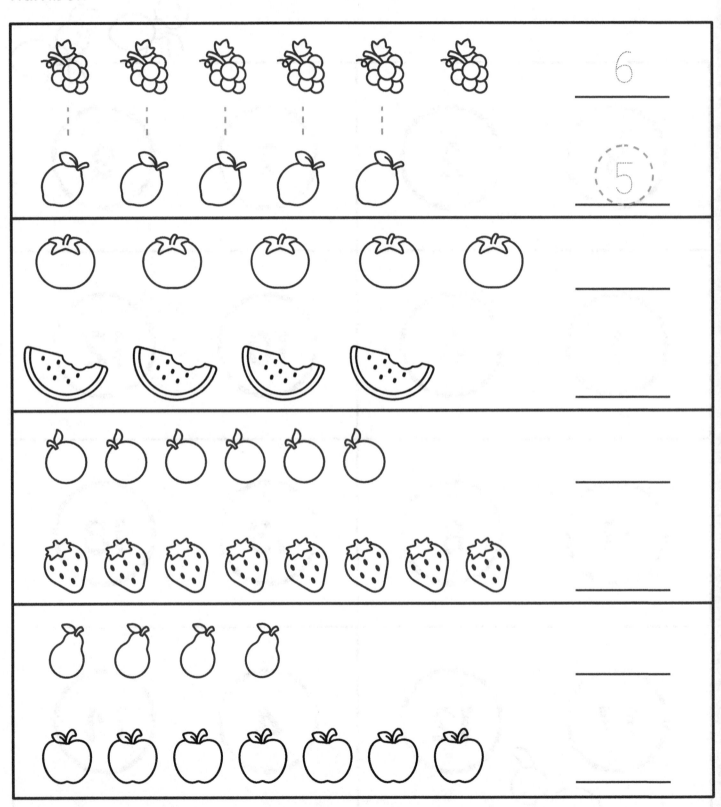

Comparing Numbers   53

Count the objects in each group. Write the number on the line. Circle the **SMALLER** number in each pair.

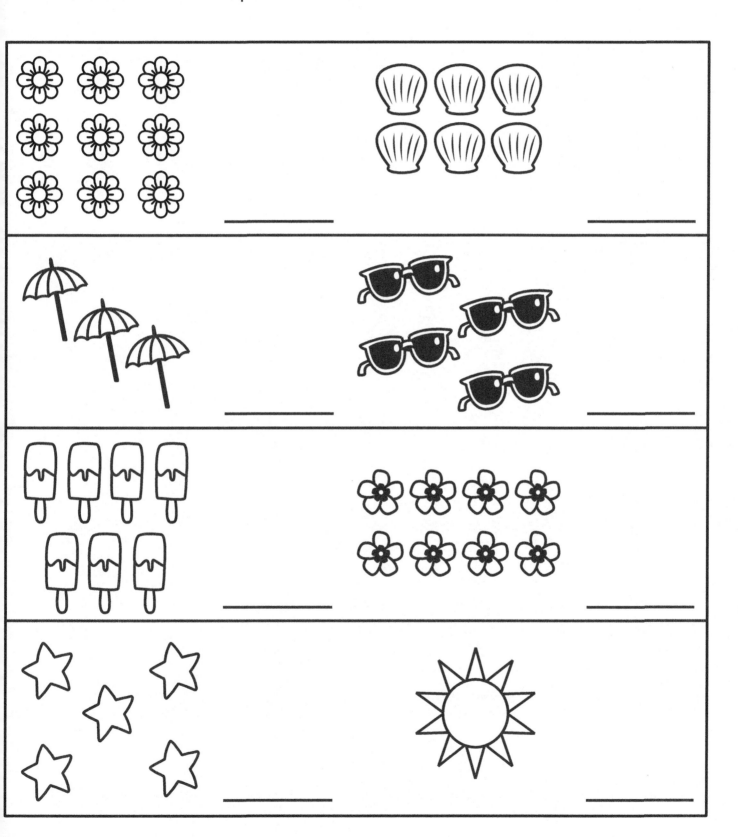

UNIT 2

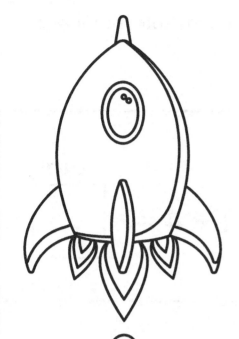

Operations

- Skill 1: Addition .... p. 56
- Skill 2: Subtraction .... p. 64
- Skill 3: Mixed Operations .... p. 70

56 — Addition

Color the crayons red and blue as directed. Then write the total number of crayons in the box.

Color **1** red and **4** blue.

1 + 4 =   Total

Color **2** red and **1** blue.

2 + 1 =   Total

Color **5** red and **2** blue.

5 + 2 =   Total

Color **4** red and **0** blue.

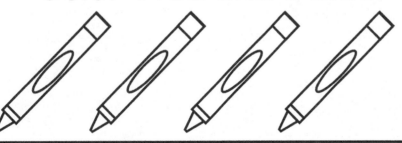

4 + 0 =   Total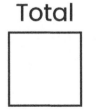

Addition

57

Count the number of treats in each group and write the number in the box below. Then, add to find the total and complete the equation.

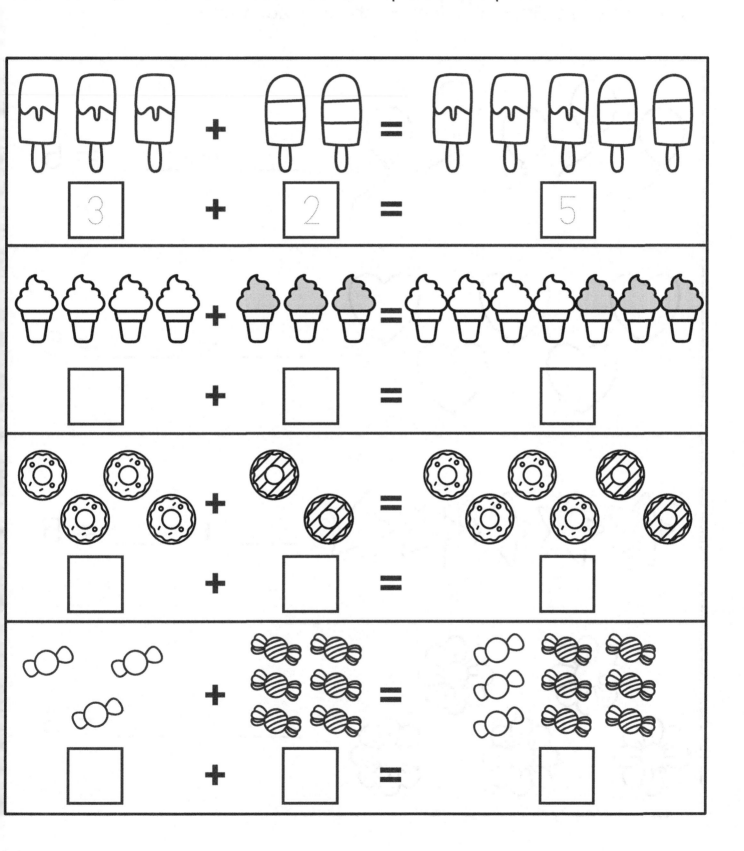

58 | Addition

In each set, color some of the objects with one color and the rest with another color. Fill in the equation with the correct numbers to show how you made five. Use a different pair of numbers for each set.

___ + ___ = 5

___ + ___ = 5

___ + ___ = 5

___ + ___ = 5

Addition

59

Draw more seeds on each watermelon to make a total of 10. Write the number on the line to complete the equation.

4 + ___ = 10

6 + ___ = 10

7 + ___ = 10

5 + ___ = 10

3 + ___ = 10

2 + ___ = 10

60 Addition

Count the dots and write the number next to the domino. Then, add to find the total number of dots on each domino.

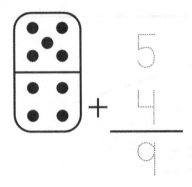 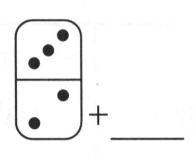 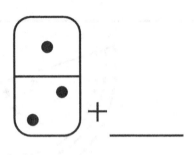

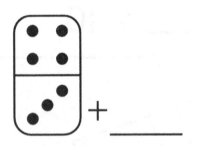 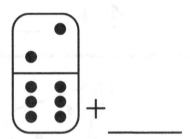

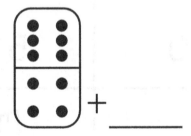

Addition

61

Draw a picture to help you solve each addition equation.

3 + 2 = ___	1 + 2 = ___
4 + 3 = ___	7 + 1 = ___
2 + 4 = ___	5 + 3 = ___

62 Addition

Read each word problem. Draw a picture in the box, then fill in the numbers to complete the equation.

Tina picks 3 red apples and 4 green apples. How many apples does she pick all together?

____ + ____ = ____

Ben has 2 green toy cars and 4 blue toy cars. How many toy cars does he have in all?

____ + ____ = ____

Mia has 3 brothers and 1 sister. How many brothers and sisters does she have?

____   ____   ____

Addition

63

Find each sum.

5	1	2	5	5
+ 3	+ 2	+ 3	+ 4	+ 5
8				

2	6	3	2	4
+ 7	+ 4	+ 3	+ 4	+ 1

3	5	1	6	6
+ 4	+ 1	+ 9	+ 3	+ 1

2	8	1	3	8
+ 6	+ 2	+ 7	+ 7	+ 1

Subtraction

For each subtraction equation, cross out the correct number of objects. Then finish the equation by writing how many objects are left.

5 - 1 = 4

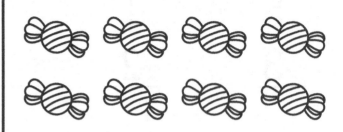

8 - 5 = ___

10 - 8 = ___

4 - 2 = ___

6 - 3 = ___

3 - 2 = ___

Subtraction

65

Each birthday cake below has some of its candles blown out. Fill in each subtraction equation to show how many candles have been blown out and how many are still lit.

5 - _3_ = _2_

4 - ___ = ___

6 - ___ = ___

3 - ___ = ___

7 - ___ = ___

2 - ___ = ___

66 Subtraction

Complete each subtraction equation using the pictures shown.

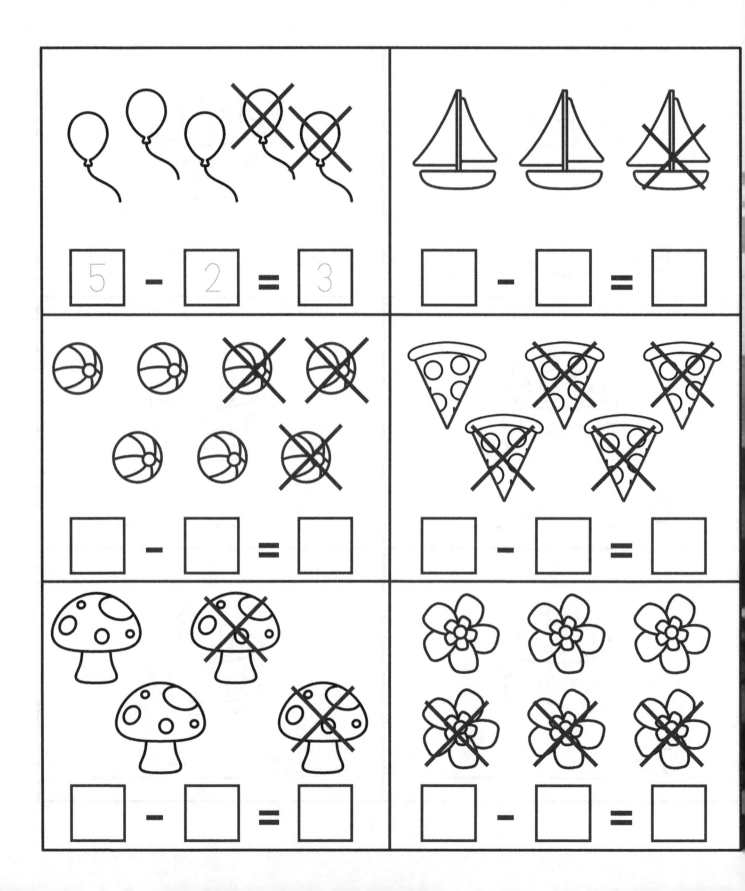

Subtraction

Draw a picture to help you solve each subtraction equation.

3 - 2 = ___	5 - 2 = ___
4 - 3 = ___	7 - 1 = ___
6 - 4 = ___	8 - 3 = ___

68 Subtraction

Read each word problem. Draw a picture in the box, then fill in the numbers to complete the equation.

Luca has 3 cookies. He gives 1 to his friend. How many cookies does he have left?

___ - ___ = ___

Ava has 6 lit candles on her birthday cake. She blows out 3 candles. How many candles are still lit?

___ - ___ = ___

Carlos has 8 carrot sticks. He eats 4 of them. How many carrot sticks are left?

___ - ___ = ___

Subtraction

69

Find each difference.

5	10	8	6	4
− 3	− 1	− 3	− 5	− 2
2				

9	7	5	3	2
− 2	− 4	− 1	− 2	− 1

3	6	9	10	4
− 1	− 4	− 7	− 3	− 1

5	7	9	10	8
− 3	− 2	− 6	− 5	− 4

70 Mixed Operations

The numbers in the apples add up to the number in the tree. Fill in the missing numbers.

Mixed Operations

71

Choose the equation in each group that best represents the picture.

○ 3 − 1 = 2
○ 3 + 1 = 4
○ 2 − 1 = 1

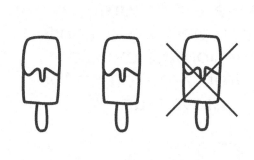

○ 6 − 4 = 2
○ 4 + 6 = 10
○ 4 + 5 = 9

○ 4 − 3 = 1
○ 3 + 2 = 5
○ 8 − 3 = 5

72 Mixed Operations

Read each word problem. Draw a picture in the box, then fill in the numbers to complete the equation.

There were 4 children on the playground. Then, 1 child went home. How many children were left on the playground?

____ ☐ ____ = ____

Anna has 3 balls. Maddie has 2 balls. How many balls do they have all together?

____ ☐ ____ = ____

Dante picked 5 flowers. Maya picked 2 flowers. How many flowers did they pick in all?

____ ☐ ____ = ____

Mixed Operations

73

Find each sum or difference.

4	1	5	1	4
− 3	+ 1	− 3	+ 2	− 2

5	2	4	3	3
− 1	+ 0	− 1	+ 2	− 1

5	3	5	1	3
− 4	+ 1	− 2	+ 4	− 2

3	2	2	2	5
− 1	+ 1	− 1	+ 2	− 5

UNIT 3

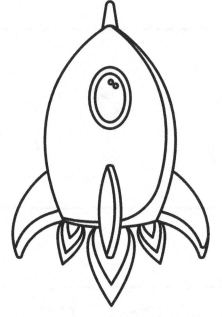

Geometry

 2-D Shapes . . . . p. 76

 3-D Shapes . . . . p. 90

2-D Shapes

Trace the circles.

Find and color the circles.

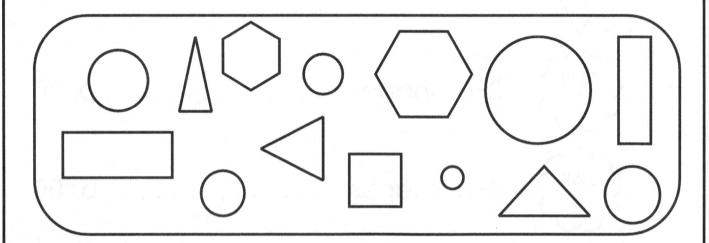

Draw 3 circles below.

Circles have _____ corners.

2-D Shapes

Trace the triangles.

Find and color the triangles.

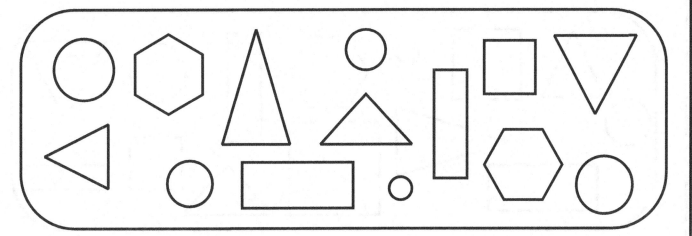

Draw 3 triangles below.

Triangles have _____ sides and corners.

2-D Shapes

Trace the squares.

Find and color the squares.

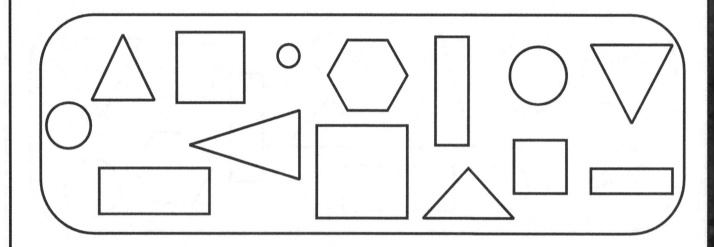

Draw 3 squares below.

Squares have _____ sides and corners.

2-D Shapes

Trace the rectangles.

Find and color the rectangles.

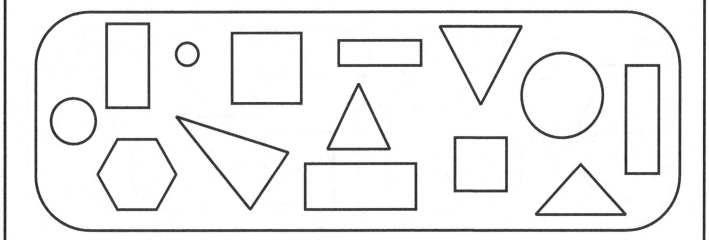

Draw 3 rectangles below.

Rectangles have _____ sides and corners.

2-D Shapes

Trace the pentagons.

Find and color the pentagons.

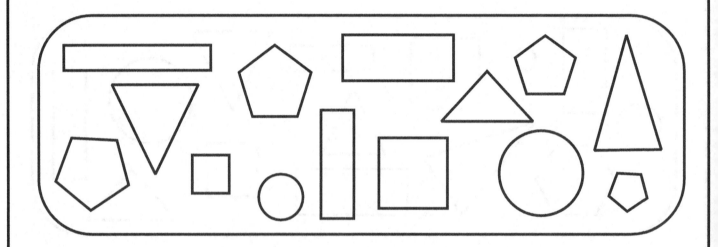

Draw 3 pentagons below.

Pentagons have _____ sides and corners.

2-D Shapes

81

Trace the hexagons.

Find and color the hexagons.

Draw 3 hexagons below.

Hexagons have _____ sides and corners.

2-D Shapes

Write the number of sides each shape has inside the shape.

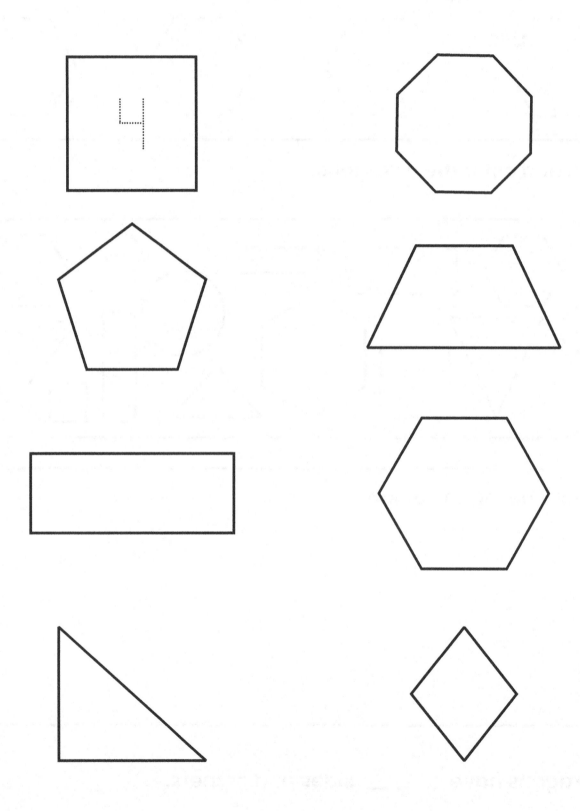

2-D Shapes

83

Color the shapes that have the same number of sides as the first shape in each row.

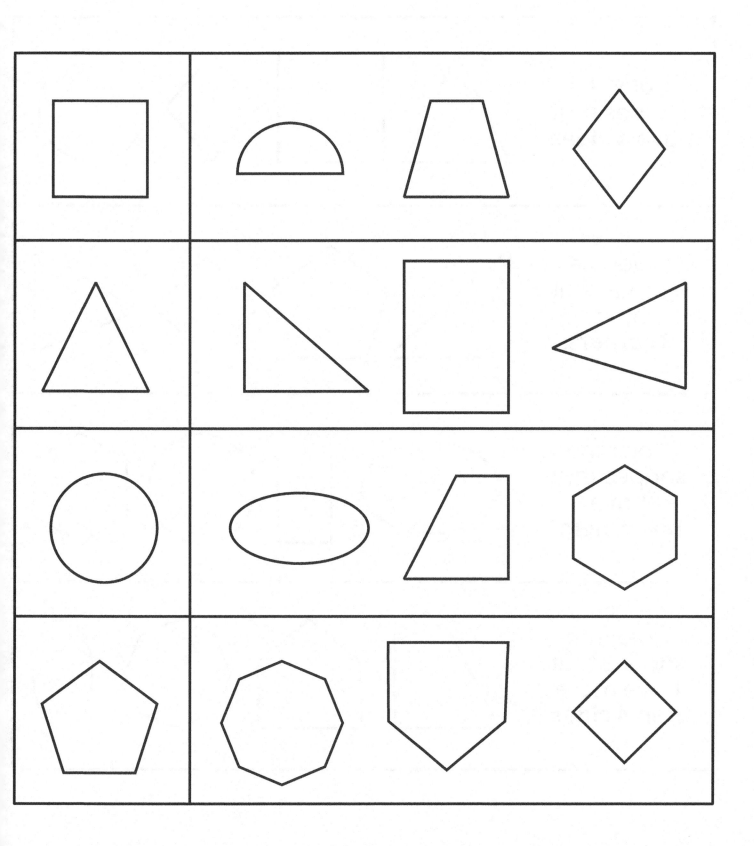

2-D Shapes

Color the shapes that match the description in each row.

Color the shapes that have **4 sides**.	△ ☐ ◇ ◯
Color the shapes that have **3 corners**.	◺ ⬠ ◇ ◁
Color the shapes that have **no corners**.	⬭ ▯ ◯ ⬡
Color the shapes that have **more than 4 sides**.	trapezoid, pentagon (house), nonagon, oval

2-D Shapes

85

Color all the **TRIANGLES** to make a path from start to finish.

86 | 2-D Shapes

Color each **SQUARE** — RED

Color each **CIRCLE** — BLUE

Color each **TRIANGLE** — GREEN

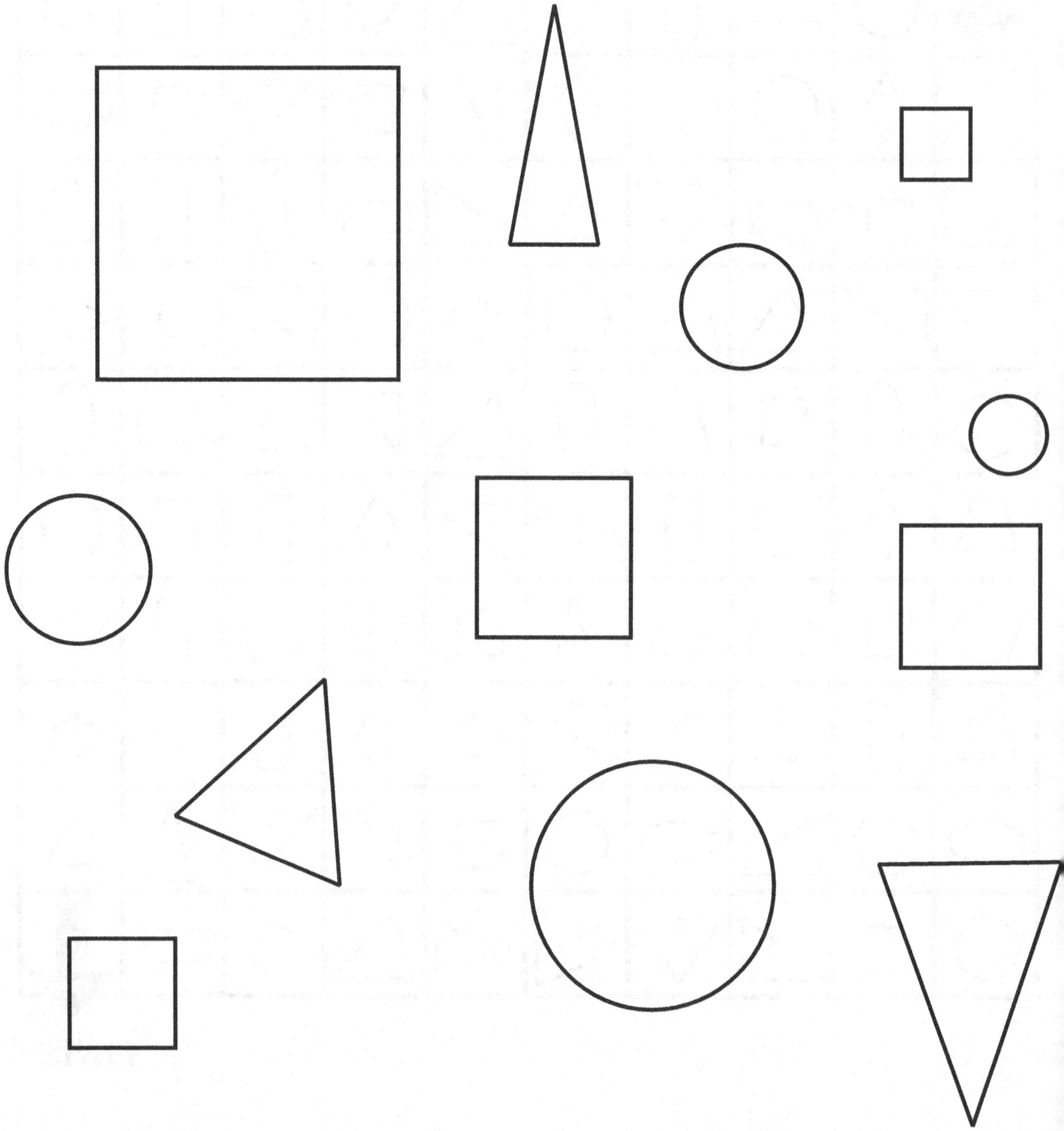

2-D Shapes

87

Color the pictures that match the first shape in each row.

2-D Shapes

Draw lines to create smaller shapes inside each shape shown.

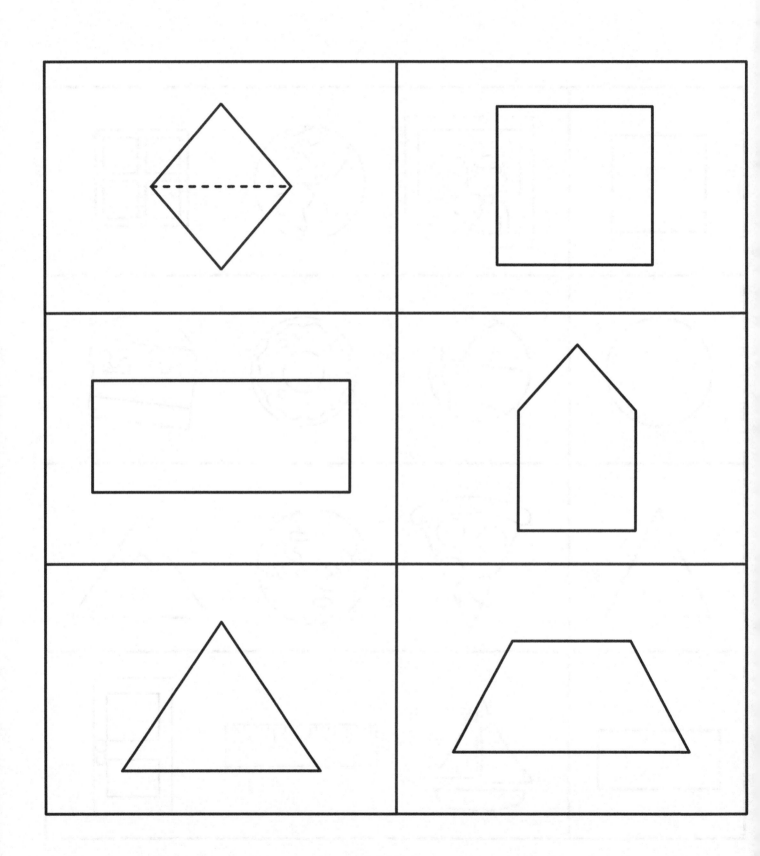

2-D Shapes

89

Use the two shapes shown to create a new, larger shape.

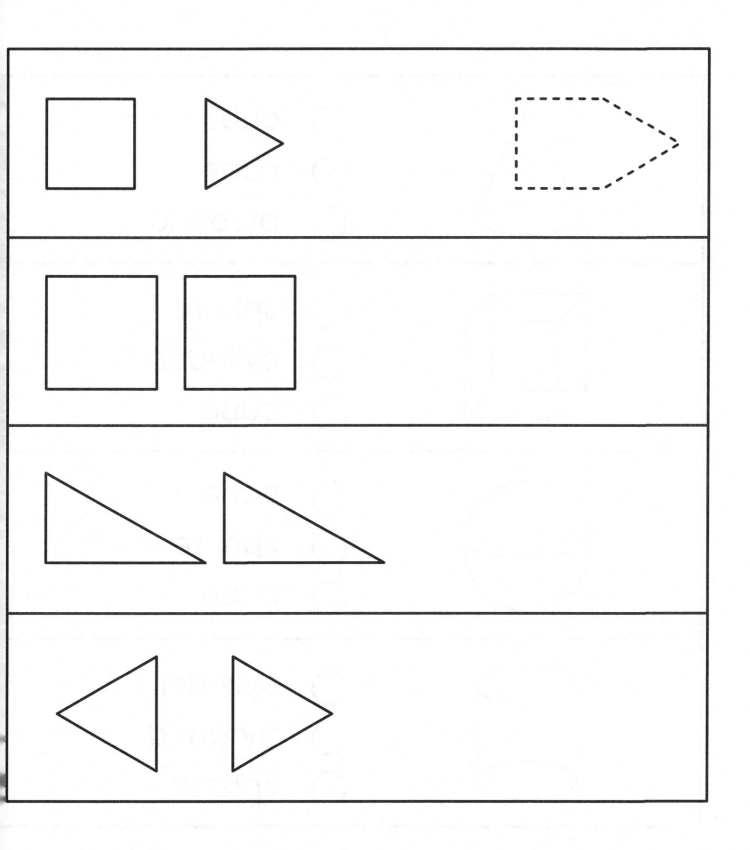

| 90 | 3-D Shapes |

Fill in the circle to show the correct name of each solid (3-D) shape shown.

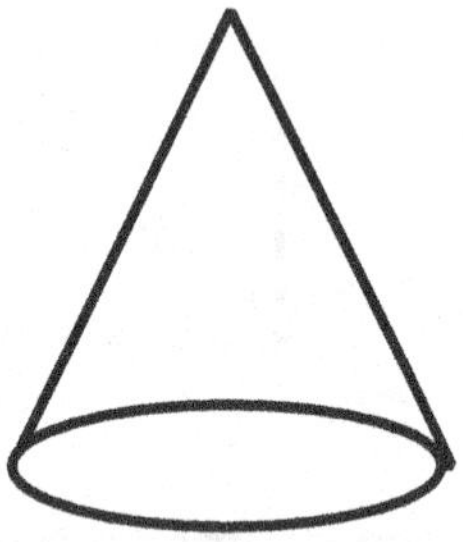

- ○ cube
- ○ cone
- ○ pyramid

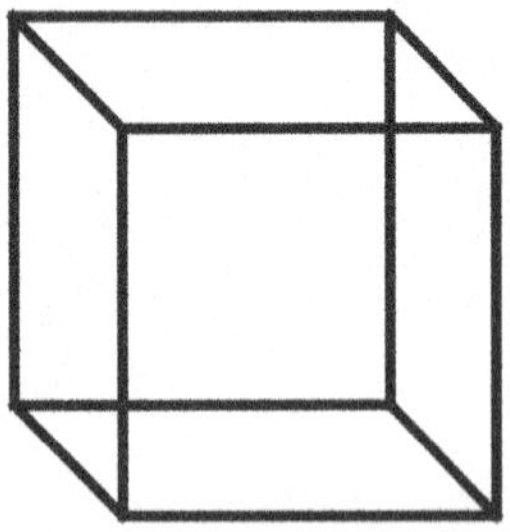

- ○ sphere
- ○ cylinder
- ○ cube

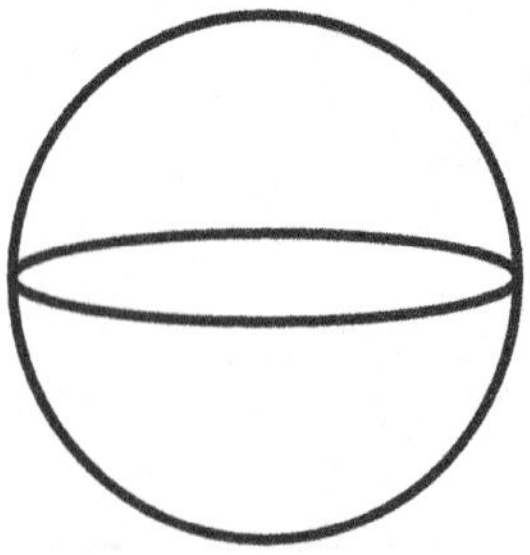

- ○ cone
- ○ sphere
- ○ cube

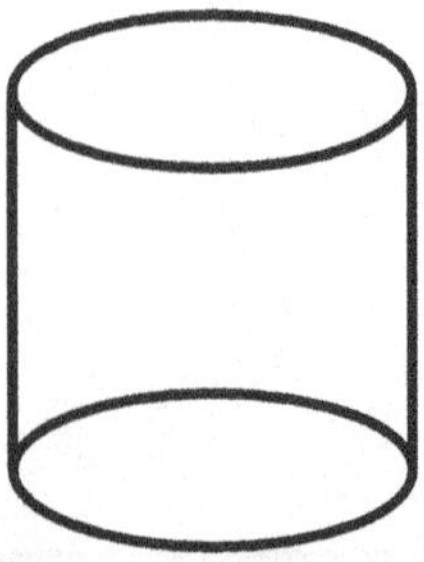

- ○ cylinder
- ○ pyramid
- ○ sphere

3-D Shapes

Circle the correct 3-D shape in each group.

Which shape is a **sphere**?	
Which shape is a **cube**?	
Which shape is a **cylinder**?	
Which shape is a **pyramid**?	

3-D Shapes

Circle the solid (3-D) shape that matches the description in each row.

Circle the solid figure that has **only flat surfaces**.

Circle the solid figure that has **only curved surfaces**.

Circle the solid figure that has **both flat and curved surfaces**.

Circle the solid figure that has **only flat surfaces that are all the same size**.

3-D Shapes

Color the flat (2-D) shapes **RED** and the solid (3-D) shapes **BLUE**.

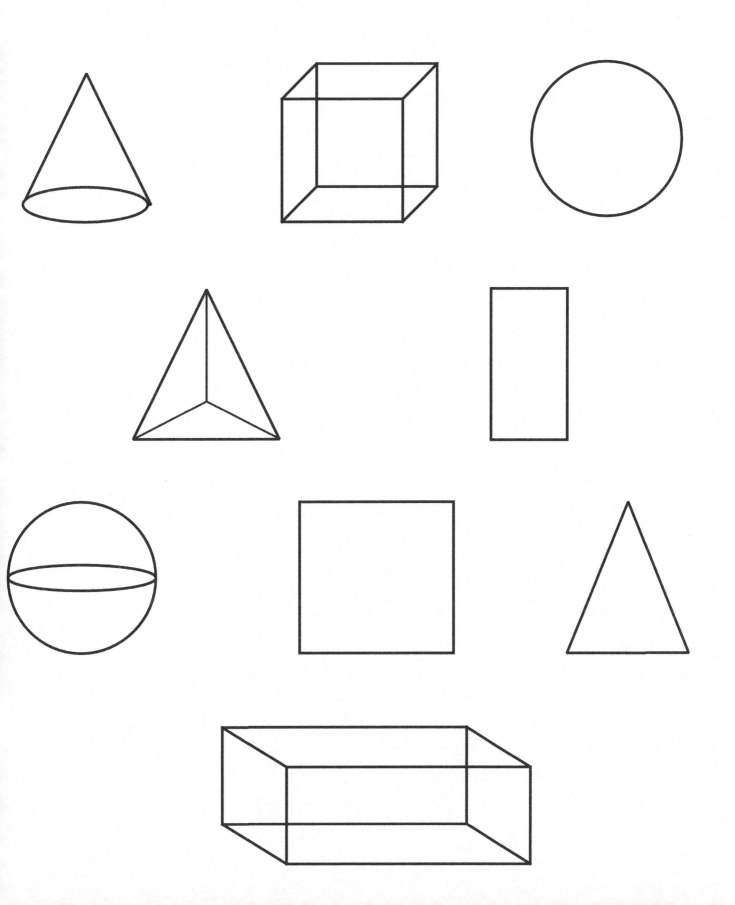

UNIT 4

Measurement and Data

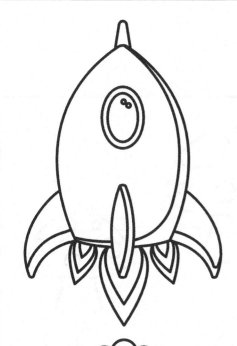

- Skill 1 Size . . . . p. 96
- Skill 2 Position . . . . p. 100
- Skill 3 Sorting and Classifying . . . . . . p. 102
- Skill 4 Ordering . . . . p. 106

Size

Color the object in each pair that is **BIGGER**.

Size

97

In each box are several shapes. Some are big and some are small. Count how many shapes are big and how many are small.

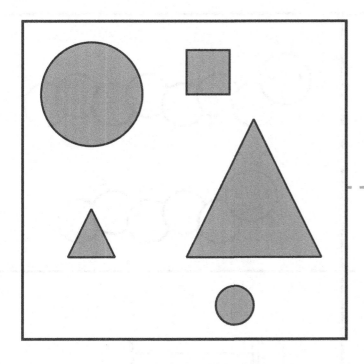

How many shapes are **BIG**?

_____ shapes

How many shapes are **SMALL**?

_____ shapes

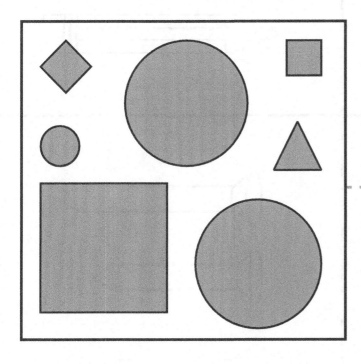

How many shapes are **BIG**?

_____ shapes

How many shapes are **SMALL**?

_____ shapes

98 Size

In each pair, color the object that is **LONGER**.

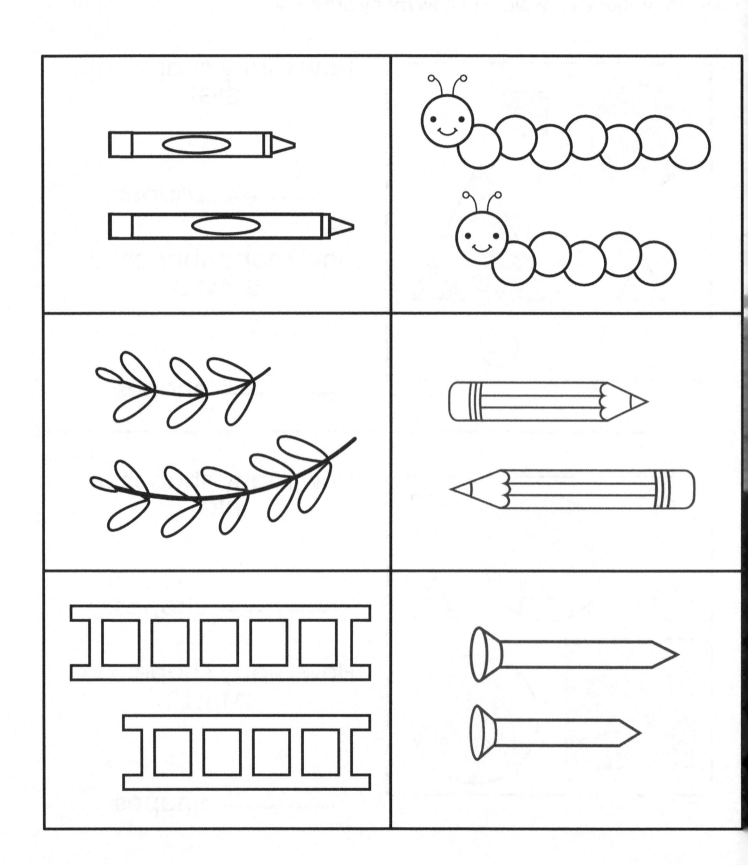

Size

In each pair, color the object that is **SHORTER**.

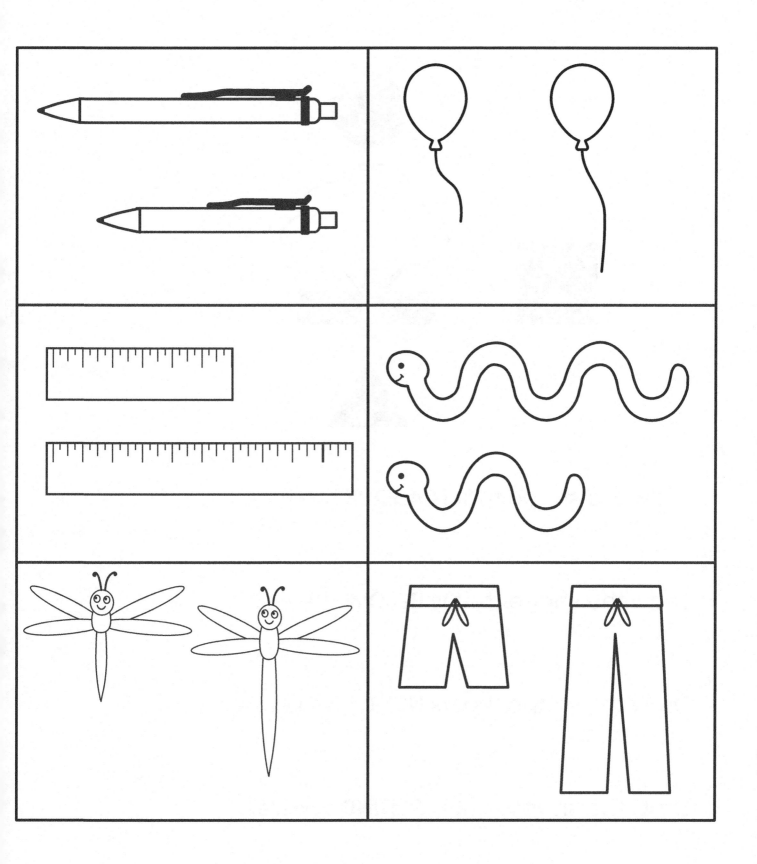

100 Position

Answer each question about the shapes pictured below.

Draw the shape that is **ABOVE** the tree.

Draw the shape that is **BELOW** the tree.

Draw the shape that is **NEXT TO** the tree.

Draw the shape that is **BEHIND** the tree.

Position

101

Write or draw the correct shape to complete each sentence.

The _____ is **behind** the _____.	The _____ is **in front of** the _____.
The _____ is **below** the _____.	The _____ is **above** the _____.
The _____ is **to the left of** the _____.	The _____ is **to the right of** the _____.
The _____ is **over** the _____.	The _____ is **under** the _____.

102 Sorting and Classifying

There are 5 circles in the box below. Count the number of circles of each color. Draw the correct number of circles in each column, then write the number at the bottom.

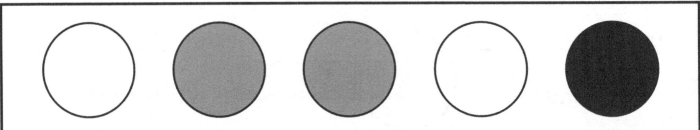

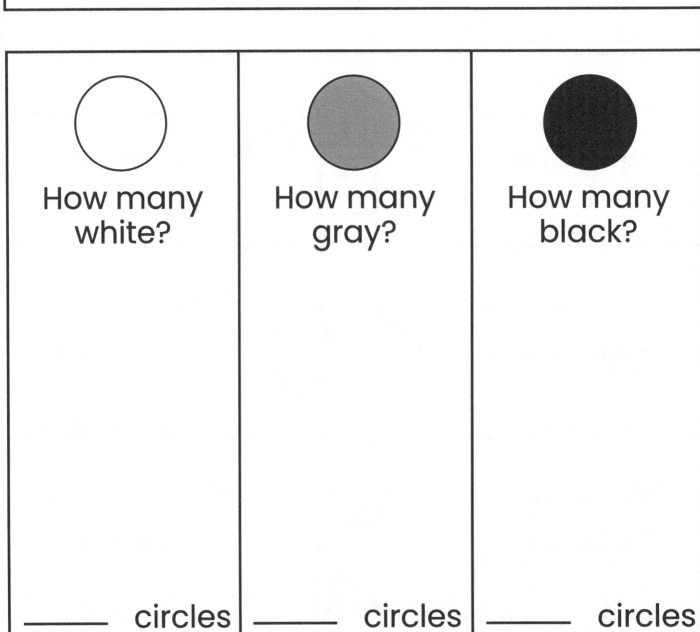

How many white?

How many gray?

How many black?

_____ circles   _____ circles   _____ circles

Sorting and Classifying

103

Count the number of each object shown and write the number in each box.

How many?

104 Sorting and Classifying

Count the number of each shape. Graph these numbers by coloring in the correct number of boxes for each shape.

Sorting and Classifying

105

Count the number of each type of bug. Graph these numbers by coloring in the correct number of boxes for each bug.

6					
5					
4					
3					
2					
1					
0	🐞	🦋	🐜	🐝	🐛

Ordering

106

In each group, number the objects from shortest (1) to tallest (5).

Ordering

107

Kate found snails in her garden. The picture below shows the snails in a line, in order by number. Answer each question about the snails.

Kate named the snails in her garden. Sookie is number 2. Coco is number 4. Ed is in line before Coco and after Sookie. What number is Ed?

① ② ③ ④ ⑤

- -

If Kate found another snail and added it to the end of the line, what number would that snail be? Write the number in the box.

Made in the USA
Monee, IL
22 March 2024